Does God Answer?

Carroll E. Simcox

Inter-Varsity Press

INTER-VARSITY PRESS
38 De Montfort Street, Leicester LE1 7GP, England

© 1985 by Inter-Varsity Christian Fellowship of the United States of America.

All rights reserved. No part of this publication may be reproduced, stored in a retrieval system, or transmitted, in any form or by any means, electronic, mechanical, photocopying, recording or otherwise without the prior permission of Inter-Varsity Press.

All quotations from Scripture, unless otherwise noted, are taken from the King James Version of the Bible.

First published 1985

British Library Cataloguing in Publication Data

Simcox, Carroll E.
  Does God answer?
  1. Prayer
  I. Title
  248.3'2   BV210.2

  ISBN 0–85110–471–1

Typeset in the United States of America

Printed in Great Britain by Cox & Wyman Ltd, Reading

Inter-Varsity Press is the publishing division of the Universities and Colleges Christian Fellowship (formerly the Inter-Varsity Fellowship), a student movement linking Christian Unions in universities and colleges throughout the United Kingdom and the Republic of Ireland, and a member movement of the International Fellowship of Evangelical Students. For information about local and national activities write to UCCF, 38 De Montfort Street, Leicester LE1 7GP.

A TOPICAL FOREWORD
BY ONE WHOSE VIEWS ON PRAYER
ARE SEVERELY PRAGMATIC

Miss Watson she took me in the closet and prayed, but nothing come of it. She told me to pray every day, and whatever I asked for I would get it. But it warn't so. I tried it. Once I got a fish-line, but no hooks. It warn't any good to me without hooks. I tried for the hooks three or four times, but somehow I couldn't make it work. By and by, one day, I asked Miss Watson to try for me, but she said I was a fool. She never told me why, and I couldn't make it out no way.

I set down one time back in the woods, and had a long think about it. I says to myself, if a body can get anything they pray for, why don't Deacon Winn get back the money he lost on pork? Why can't the widow get back her silver snuff-box that was stole? Why can't Miss Watson fat up? No, says I to myself, there ain't nothing in it.

HUCKLEBERRY FINN

1
The Morning
After

28 JANUARY. THIS BOOK WAS BORN last night during the sleepless hours as I lay low with flu. I believe that God gives me sleepless spells so that I will use that time praying for others. This was my second such night in a row, and I had done a lot of praying (along with a lot of absurd fantasizing about myself as I should be if I were somebody else—*vanitas vanitatum*).

My praying had been dutiful and tedious, like "Lord, I pray for poor John. He is unhappy in his work, but it's a job and jobs are scarce and he can't do anything else. You know better than I what he needs. So bless him and see him through this hard time and give him grace to grow in the knowledge and love of Thee." That's a "safe" enough prayer because it avoids the presumptuous sin of giving God good advice. I can't bring myself to tell God how to run his shop, and it seems to me that all informative and directive prayers are intended to do just that.

I reflected last night that we ought not to be troubled if our praying for others is often tedious. All worthwhile work has its drudgery as well as its ecstasy, so why shouldn't prayer? "The test of a vocation," notes Logan Pearsall Smith, "is the love of drudgery it involves."[1] I would put that somewhat differently and say that the test of a vocation is that love of its object which, in a strange paradox, makes even its drudgery a delight: "And Jacob served seven years for Rachel; and they seemed unto him but a few days, for the love he had to her" (Gen 29:20).

We expect prayers to be answered, otherwise we would not offer them. But I have never read a book on the subject of whether or not all prayers are in fact answered, and if so how. I have read many books and have heard—and preached—many sermons simply declaring that God always answers prayers, but the authors and preachers have been notably reticent about how he does so. And so as I pondered this last night, there came to me a rather imperious thought that I should tackle this job.

But what, if anything, can I say that others have not said? Of course that remains to be seen, because the book remains to be written; moreover, if our Lord never thought of being original, as George Macdonald reminded us, there is no need for his disciple to be. I claim no special access to God's secret counsels. At this point I don't know whether I can answer, or even clarify, for anybody the question of how God answers prayers, but I feel impelled to think it through as well as I can on paper. (I am one of those people who never quite know what they think until they hear or read themselves saying it.)

This morning I will put down a few preliminary reflections, then take them up later for full treatment.

Everybody who has ever prayed knows well that we don't get what we ask from God exactly how and when we want it, and that gives us our "unanswered prayer" problem. It is a false label. The fact that we don't get what we want does not mean that we get nothing, as would be the case if our prayer were unanswered. It is childish to suppose that the Perfect Parent must give us whatever we want whenever we ask him for it. But if there is any dimension of our lives in which most of us feel jubilantly free to be deliberately childish, it is our religion. (I do not say child*like*, for children normally think harder than do adults.)

The more specific and directive we are in prayer—for example, "Dear God, please heal Dad's arthritis"—the more positive we usually are that we know the only right answer to our prayer. We have given God the information he needs. If he does not come through as requested, after we have spelled it out to him so fully and clearly, what can be said for his vaunted omnicompetence? This is one of the things we must think through.

Long ago I came to the conclusion that there is no such thing as unanswered prayer, and I believe I was led to it by the Holy Spirit. If we think there is unanswered prayer, it is because we have a defective understanding of the words *prayer* and *answer*. The unanswered-prayer problem exists only for those whose conception of God is a misconception. This misconception is a twofold error, compounded by thinking about God as if he were human, which he is not, and about ourselves as if we were *merely* human, which we are not. I'll try to tell you precisely what I mean by this, once I am up to it. Victims of this misconception suppose that if God answers prayers he must do so like a mailing from supplying orders.

Most of our errors about God result from thinking about him as though he were like us. The teaching of the Bible, and of the church when it rightly divides the Word of Truth, is that God is *not* like us at all (thank God!), but that by his grace we may become like him. When we approach God with any thought that the right way is to come to him as we would any supremely wise, good and powerful man of whom we are suppliants, we are on the wrong line and dialing the wrong number. In that case God will hear our prayer and will answer it, but in a way so different from what we expect that we may not recognize it as an answer at all. Our erroneous conception of him gives us an erroneous expectation from him, and that is how our category of "unanswered prayer" gets invented.

Another truth we shall examine is expressed by Peter Kreeft: "The reason our prayers are not answered is that they are our prayers."[2] I believe that "our" prayers are in fact answered even when not as we expect or want, but Kreeft's point is right. Our theology of prayer is defective if we think that it is fundamentally or solely we who pray.

Prayer is genuine, not as something we do but as something initiated and directed in us by God. It is God in us praying to God through us as we surrender our being to him for his use. Thus prayer is essentially a divine activity rather than a human one. It is our participation in the life of God as his life is lived in and through us. (This is not to say that the divine life is lived *only* within and through us. It is being lived everywhere, hence through us.) I am astounded by the almost total lack of any such teaching in the Christian church, in all its parts, throughout past and present. Not one educated Christian in a thousand (a very conservative estimate) has ever heard that prayer is a divine activity in which God prays to God through us.

Unless I am drastically wrong about this, most people, even well-instructed Christians, uncritically assume that when they pray they do so on their own initiative rather than God's, and so they consider the action of prayer entirely their own. Nevertheless, their praying is not entirely in vain, for as they pray (or are prayed through by God) the Holy Spirit influences in some degree what they pray, making it less self-centered and more befitting a child of God. Only God knows how much of your prayer is his and how much yours, but it's always a mix of the two. When prayer passes at last into its final state of pure godliness in which God, not self, is all-in-all, it becomes that perfect adoration which is the perpetual music of heaven.

I don't want to anticipate everything we shall be thinking about in the following pages, so now I'll take my pill and crawl back into bed.

2
Who
Prays?

O ye whales, and all that move in the waters, bless ye the Lord:
praise him, and magnify him forever.
The Song of the Three Holy Children

THE WHOLE WORLD PRAYS: every living creature in it, in one
way or another.

As I write this my collie Tam is lying a few feet from me.
A dog has its own way of knowing God, and Tam worships
God in the manner God has appointed for his canine creatures. I have observed him in at least part of his worship. He
says his grace regularly, though after meals rather than before.
This may be due to some streak of Scottish canniness in him
by which he reasons that it is not prudent to give thanks in
advance for a dinner you may not like. After his dinner he
comes into the living room, lies on his back, rolls around

growling ecstatically and saying with his body language something I translate as, "My God, that was magnificent chow! And thanks especially for adding those table scraps of macaroni and cheese."

"The young lions roar after their prey, and seek their meat from God" (Ps 104:21). Their roar is the same as our prayer for our daily bread. All the world prays, and all prayer is good, but to that must be added, in Orwellian phrase, that all prayers are equal but some are more equal than others.

There is a categorical distinction between two kinds of prayer: creaturely and filial. Tam and I are both creatures of God and both pray as creatures. I do that when I pray for my daily bread or ask God to keep our home in peace and safety through the night. But I am also a child of God in a sense that Tam is not.[1] God through Christ has adopted me to be an heir of his kingdom and to share with him the work of his continuing creation and government of his world. He has given me a kind of deputed dominion over my dog, but it is really his dominion to be exercised through me, and I am answerable to him for any failure to govern his beloved creature as he would have me do. Tam experiences God's love and care for him largely through my hands.

The realization of this must have a profoundly influential bearing on my praying. I am called to pray in a threefold capacity—as a dependent creature of God, as a loving child of God and as a faithful agent of God in his dominion over his creation. (The fact that we have dominion over creation is a clear implication of all the parables of Jesus about stewardship.) The Spirit moves me to pray in these three capacities, and as I surrender to the Spirit my prayer becomes filial without ceasing to be creaturely. "Give us this day our daily bread" is creaturely; "Thy kingdom come" is filial.

The lion's creaturely prayer is not inferior to the saint's filial prayer; each prays appropriately after his own kind—that is, according to the will of God for him. Indeed, all truly inferior prayers are offered by human beings because our species has fallen out of its proper relationship with God and hence with itself. St. Paul was keenly aware of our human infirmity in prayer: "We know not what we should pray for as we ought" (Rom 8:26). The dog doesn't need to be taught to pray, nor does the whale, nor the oak tree; it does so as naturally as it eats and breathes. The creature's prayer is the expression of its dependence on God. It is implicit in the creature's very being. We too have this sense of dependence implicit in our being, but as we now are it is warped by our illusion of self-sufficiency.

One can define prayer so broadly as to identify it, quite simply, with desire. Under such a definition the atheist prays whenever he wants something, and it is valid as creaturely prayer. But if there is nothing in it except wanting something, it falls short even of the prayer in my dog's grace after meals, in which there is an ecstasy of pleasure and gratitude for blessings received. Prayer that is *only* desire is one of the beggarly rudiments, so beggarly that its right to be called prayer is questionable.

When his first followers asked Jesus to teach them to pray, we don't know what they expected, but we know what he gave them: the Lord's Prayer (Mt 6:9-13; Lk 11:1-4). Its salutation, *Our Father,* tells us that Christ sees prayer as an expression not only of creaturely need but of filial love for God. He sees God not only as our Maker but as our Father, and he teaches us to see God so. Christ himself "became what we are in order to make us what He is."[2] The model prayer he gives us is meant to set our feet in the way that leads to that exalted end. For all who live in Christ, prayer is the beginning of their eternal life with God.

The prayer of simple creaturely desire is natural prayer. Prayer in Christ does not cease to be natural but becomes supernatural because of what is added from above to our ordinary, natural creaturely being: the knowledge of God as our Father and of ourselves as his adopted children. The word *supernatural* has suffered a sad and unjust fate in being commonly associated with the occult, the spooky, ghosts, poltergeists and other such things. But it is a decent word deserving decent usage. A person is born naturally in his or her mother's womb, then may be given a second birth supernaturally by the Holy Spirit. Praying in Christ is supernatural through and through.

Jesus tells us that whatever we ask of the Father in his name God will give us (Jn 15:16). Such a phrase as *in Christ's name* or *through Jesus Christ our Lord* is not a password or magical formula, although it is all too commonly so used by Christians who should know better. In biblical usage the name of God is another way of saying the being of God. Christ is God in our humanity, so to pray in his name is to pray with him and in him. To approach God in Christ's name is to do so as living members of him, and this incredible and truly supernatural thing we can do because he invites and enables us to do it.

C. S. Lewis describes this mystery with his usual clarity. Speaking of the words *Our Father* he says:

They mean quite frankly that you are putting yourself in the place of a son of God. To put it bluntly, you are *dressing up as Christ.* If you like, you are pretending. Because, of course, you realize that you are not a son of God. You are not a being like The Son of God, whose will and interests are at one with those of the Father: you are a bundle of self-centred fears, hopes, greeds, jealousies, and self-conceit. So that, in a way, this dressing up as Christ is a piece of out-rageous cheek. But the odd thing is that He has ordered us to do it.[3]

Lewis goes on to say that our initial pretending is the very thing God will use to turn our pretense into reality, and as we pray in Christ that is what he is actually doing with us. We are already sons and daughters of God as we grow in grace, increasingly sharing with God our Father and Christ our Brother the character of the divine family into which we have been adopted.

The most mature filial prayers can all be spoken in one word: *Abba.* The whole sum of what Jesus teaches us about prayer, and indeed about God, is in that untranslatable Aramaic word which he teaches us to use. It is a dialect word meaning "my Father" and containing a note of affection mingled with awe that makes straight translation into English impossible; we have no corresponding word. *Daddy* won't do, because although it expresses affection, it does not express the awe and holy fear which must characterize our feeling toward God.[4] *Abba* is the infinitely great Maker and Ruler of the universe who is also the infinitely tender Lord and Lover of his children and his creatures.

"Because ye are sons, God hath sent forth the Spirit of his Son into your hearts, crying, Abba, Father" (Gal 4:6). I once read a sermon by a minister who recalled how one day he sat at his study desk working on next Sunday's sermon when he was aware that his small son had entered the room. "What do you want, son?" he asked. The lad quavered as he answered, "Nothing. I just want to be with you." There was the spirit of pure prayer crying "Abba." The essence of filial prayer, prayer in Christ, is fellowship with God—just being with him. God is always present with us; filial prayer is making ourselves present to him—if you will, calling his attention to us and calling our own attention to him.

Everybody, everything prays. Christ raises us to the prayer that cries "Abba," and thus we make our infantile beginning of that being "with Christ in God" (Col 3:3) which is our eternal life.

3
That Mischievous Misconception

God made no tools for himself, he needs none;
he created himself a partner in the dialogue of time,
and one who is capable of holding converse with him.
Martin Buber

I NOW FEEL UP TO tackling the subject of that twofold misconception about God and ourselves which I mentioned on the morning after. The misconception consists of thinking anthropologically about God and *not* thinking theologically about ourselves. We think about God as if he were human—that is the first part of the mistake; and the second part of it is our thinking about ourselves as though we were only human creatures, rather than seeing ourselves as human creatures made in the image of God to be his partners in the dialog of time, capable of holding converse with him. We think too humanly about God and not divinely enough about ourselves when we commit this error, and as it possesses our minds it perverts our praying.

To pray rightly we must have a right understanding about God and a right understanding about ourselves. A right understanding about God is not knowing all about him. Knowing all about God is neither possible for us nor required of us as his creatures. Such knowledge will have to wait until we are ushered into heaven, and our direct exploration of the unfathomable shining depths of God will only begin in that moment when we see him face to face. For our present stage of life it is enough that we know God as *Abba*. Even this, however, is a real beginning of growth in a true knowledge of God as he is. Prayer in Christ always brings growth in authentic knowledge and love of God.

A right understanding of ourselves consists of a thoroughly realistic knowledge that we are animal creatures of God along with the dogs and apes and slugs and crabs, and also that we are immortal souls for whom Christ was willing to die so that he could raise us to a whole new dimension of life in himself. And so our praying, if it is to be what God wants it to be, will be both creaturely and filial.

To whatever extent the mischievous misconception governs our minds, it prevents our praying in Christ and our growth in him. I still have trouble shaking it off from my own mind, though I have been theologically aware of its falsehood for many years, and once I've shaken it off I have trouble keeping it "shook off." I assume that others have the same trouble, and so for the next several chapters we shall examine some of the errors about prayer which in one way or another stem from this misconception.

24

We may begin with the idea of prayer which, in essence, sees prayer as a power or force, a pressure tactic, that we can wield in order to get what we want. We may call it *Pelagian prayer*. Pelagius was a British monk of sixteen centuries ago who believed that if you want to be good, all you have to do is to make up your mind—then be it. Do you drink too much? Then quit. Are you short on courage? Then be braver. You don't need the grace of God to enable you, only the guts and gumption you already have. When the Pelagian prays, he is quite sure that he is doing it all by himself. He is exercising "prayer power" and heartily believing that "prayer works."

You may have noticed that such phrases are widely used today. The heresy of Pelagius walks about in our land seeking whom it may devour, and finding many. The statement that "prayer works" is not just shorthand for "God works through prayer." It says that there is power, *mana,* in prayer itself, a force we can wield to our own purposes. Logically analyzed and candidly considered, it can only be seen as a pressure tactic intended to force God's hand to do what we want done.

Here is a bit of Pelagian prose from a widely read book on prayer by a famous scientist: "Prayer is the most powerful form of energy one can generate. The influence of prayer on the human mind and body is as demonstrable as that of the secreting glands. Prayer is a force as real as terrestrial gravity. It supplies us with a flow of sustaining power in our daily lives."[1] According to this, when we pray it is we, not God, who generate this "powerful form of energy," and the decision as to how to use it is ours, not God's.

In my own acquaintance with them I find that the people who think and pray this way are mostly very nice people—nicer than I should expect them to be if all I knew about them was their idea of "prayer power." Possibly one thing that keeps them as nice as they are is that in all their effort to wield their prayer power, it doesn't work for them most of the time, and their failure keeps them humble—or at least not inwardly sure of themselves—despite their outward confidence in their way of praying. I venture that God seldom—indeed, never—yields to their pressure tactic, because in his mercy he hopes they will grow discouraged and then radically rethink the whole matter.

The Pelagian premise is that God has given us the power to get what we want for ourselves regardless of what he wants for us. If that were true, it would mean that God has given us power over himself. The pagan Virgil is closer to the truth about prayer than is the Pelagian Christian: *Desine fata deum flecti sperare precando* ("Quit hoping that heaven's decrees can be deflected by your prayer").[2]

If we pray seriously *Thy will be done,* we see that Christian praying does not in any way seek to make our own will and wish at the centre of prayer. We pray Christianly only when we want what God wants and nothing else; or, if we do want something else, we honestly present our wish to God with the proviso that if it isn't what he wants, we don't want it either. It is always a helpful prelude to prayer to reflect on these two topics: what I want, or think that I want, and what I think God may want. We receive our instruction on the mind and will of God from meditating on Christ, in whom we meet the Father. Such a prelude, whether for a moment or an hour, may well make the difference between a Christian prayer and a Pelagian prayer, and if it does it is time well spent.

Last week a young friend asked me to keep him in my prayers because he has a job interview coming up. If it goes well for him, he will be in a much more lucrative job than his present one. I am so praying. But it's quite possible that the new job could do him more harm than good. I don't know, but God does. As I pray about it I am trying to approach God as his child with a concern for his other child, aware that it is a matter of concern to the whole Family in heaven and earth: to God and his angels and all souls in paradise, as well as to my friend and me. I can properly say to God, "I hope he gets it, but only you know what's best for him and for all others concerned, including those others who want the job."

Well then, what's the point in my praying about it at all? A fair question, but I could reasonably refer the questioner to the only One who could fully answer it. God teaches us to pray for one another but not to try to impose our will upon him or to instruct him on his duty. We are to pray for one another because he is our Father, we are his children, and as a loving family we bear one another's burdens.

Grant all that. But two questions remain. First, will my friend get the job or won't he? And second, will my prayer make any difference one way or the other? Ten years ago I think I would not have been satisfied with the answers I now give to these two questions. I am satisfied now, and I hope this means simply that the Holy Spirit has got something accomplished with my not very malleable mind.

To the first question I answer: If my friend does not get the job, it won't be because I failed to work "prayer power" to good effect, but because God mercifully delivered him from some harm which only God could foresee.

To the question as to what difference, if any, my prayer will have made, there are two answers, a negative and a positive. First, in no way will my prayer prove to have been successful in pressuring God to change his mind and his action, and for that I thank God. My batting average as a maker of wise decisions is so low that it is mercifully invisible to anybody except God. It is of his everlasting charity that even as he patiently listens he firmly overrules all human recommendations that conflict with his perfect wisdom. To be sure, "the effectual fervent prayer of a righteous man availeth much" (Jas 5:16). The fervent prayer of even an unrighteous person always avails to open the pray-er's life to the Holy Spirit, and there can be no greater gift than that gift. On the positive side, my prayer for my friend (or for my enemy) will have made a difference for the better in me. Every prayer for another is an irreversible growth in love in the one who offers it, and thus a contribution to his or her eternal life. That difference is something we can even now see and sense, but our present vision is as nothing compared to the vision that God will give us when he has fully raised us from pre-Life to Life.

Prayer itself changes nothing. God through our prayer changes everything to accord with his perfect and all-prevailing will. To see the completion of anything that God ever begins in us as prayer, we must wait for that End in which, as St. Augustine beautifully put it, *vacabimus et videbimus, videbimus et amabimus, amabimus et laudabimus* ("We shall rest and we shall see, we shall see and we shall love, we shall love and we shall praise").[3] We shall see the travail of our souls and be satisfied (Is 53:11).

4
Vain
Repetitions

Words are the most powerful drugs used by mankind.
Rudyard Kipling

W HEN YE PRAY, USE not vain repetitions, as the heathen do: for they think that they shall be heard for their much speaking. Be not ye therefore like unto them: for your Father knoweth what things ye have need of, before ye ask him" (Mt 6:7-8). Alas, if only the heathen had a monopoly of "much speaking" in prayer, thinking to be heard because of it! But they share the practice with many otherwise well-intentioned Christians. Jesus knew that it would be a temptation and a snare to his followers. It is all so human. Not only when we pray but in all our efforts to communicate we assume, as if by instinct, that the more we repeat some word or phrase or slogan, the better we are going to be deeply and soundly heard. If we are wise, we remember Calvin Coolidge with admiration for his spectacular transcendence of that thoroughly false and harmful assumption.

The text quoted above is one of the Master's most valuable teachings on prayer, and it seems to be one of the least heeded by his disciples of past and present. The Christian churches, with the exception of the Society of Friends, pour forth repetitions of prayer in an endless stream, as do most Christians in their private prayers. I have questioned people whom I knew well enough to feel free to ask about their praying, and not a few of them tell me that each night, if they say nothing else to God they say the "Now I lay me" prayer. Grown people—fifty, sixty, seventy years old, still parroting their baby prayer!

I will not say that oft-repeated prayers are necessarily vain in the sense of futile, to no effect. Only God knows what God does with them. My point is that whether our prayers are to be vain or not is not up to them but up to us. In our corporate praying unquestionably there is need for forms of prayer that will be familiar to all the worshipers. But whether we are praying alone or with a thousand others, we must realize that we can mouth prayer formulas because they relieve us of the necessity of thinking what to say to God. Such thoughtless speaking is vain repetition. Jesus teaches that if we think to be heard for our much speaking, we deceive ourselves. Such "praying" is no better than cranking forth our petitions from a wheel as do some Tibetan Buddhists.

No prayer is so thoughtlessly, hence vainly, repeated as is the prayer perfect which Jesus gave us as a pattern for our praying: a pattern, not a patter. When two or three of us are gathered in his name, we commonly feel that we must recite together the Lord's Prayer if nothing else, and we dutifully recite it—which virtually guarantees that we shall not pray it. We *cannot* pray it in a minute or so.

Frederick Denison Maurice said that we can commit the Lord's Prayer to memory very quickly, but it is slowly learned by heart. It takes, in fact, a whole lifetime to learn it by heart. Jesus did not say, "When you pray, say this." He said, "Pray in this way" (Mt 6:9). He means that this prayer is to be the framework within which our praying is to be done. It should not surprise us that when Christians are asked to set down in writing what goes through their minds as they say the Lord's Prayer, many of them fall to babbling. Nothing goes through their minds! They have never thought it through before, they do not think as they pray it now, and that is because they were not taught by their pastors and masters to think it—only to say it, and a prayer not thought is a prayer not prayed.

If you will devote a week to offering the Lord's Prayer, giving the entire first day to *Our Father* and reflecting that (1) he is our Father, not just our Maker, and (2) he is *our* Father, not just *your* Father, then go on from there at the same pace and the same concentration throughout the prayer and the week, you will realize as never before the preciousness of the Lord's gift of this prayer. It will be the most fruitful one-week "school of prayer" you could possibly attend.

When do repetitions in prayer become vain, or what makes them vain? It is not the frequency and regularity with which they are offered, but the mindlessness and carelessness with which we grind them out. There are many wonderful prayers composed by great masters of prayer which we can make our own, and when we do make them our own they will not be vain repetitions at all: they will be a sharing in the treasures of Christ's household, the riches of his family.

But we must be constantly on guard against secondhand praying in which we merely recite prayers borrowed from others. When you pray it must be *you* in conversation with God—you, nobody else. I love to offer the prayer of St. Francis which begins, "Lord, make me an instrument of Your peace." I never offer it without a strong sense that it is being answered in me as I pray. But I avoid using it routinely because even it can be made a vain repetition, and thus be nullified as prayer.

Pamela Grey once said, "For one soul that exclaims 'Speak, Lord, for thy servant heareth,' there are ten that say 'Hear, Lord! for thy servant speaketh,' and there is no rest for these."[1] If prayer is God's action in us rather than our action toward him, it is not only good manners but good sense to let him begin the action by saying whatever he wants to say to us. It won't be as if he were ringing us on the telephone; it will be wordless. When God speaks to you he speaks *through* you so intimately that, humanly and psychologically considered, it could only be described as you speaking to you. But there is a way in which we can prepare ourselves to listen to him knowing that it is indeed he who will speak to us and not just we talking to ourselves. That is by what we may call *Christic meditation,* meaning meditation "in Christ upon Christ." To fix the mind in a spirit of humble receptivity on any word or action of Jesus recorded in the Gospels, mindful that it is God Incarnate whom we are seeing and hearing, is to prepare us for what he has to say to us now. It puts us "on the same wavelength" with God as nothing else can.

You have finished your Christic meditation when you feel that God has spoken something to you through it and his word has sunk into your mind. It may sink down deeper into your subconsciousness, but no matter; through your meditation God has made you permanently more open and responsive to his guidance than before. You may be sure that henceforth when you have to make specific decisions you will be spiritually better equipped to make them with the mind of Christ in you.

Recently I read in the news about something that angered me. I instantly sat down and banged out an irate "letter to the editor" intended for publication. It was a sizzler, and as I reviewed it I rather exulted in what struck me as a most felicitous union of righteous wrath with appropriate style, remembering Luther's remark that he preached his best sermons when he was angry. "Same here!" said I to myself. But the moment I thought "wrath," God directed my mind to his word spoken through St. James: "My beloved brethren, let every man be swift to hear, slow to speak, slow to wrath: For the wrath of man worketh not the righteousness of God" (Jas 1:19-20).

I can think of at least two reasons he might have had for doing so. One was to prevent me from publishing a letter in which the wrath I expressed was not so much righteous as self-righteous. The other was that later developments showed that my initial reaction had been much overblown and was at least as wrong as it was right. I am glad that he spoke and that I listened—this time at least.

God will always show you what he wants you to do if you will listen to him through Christ. But there is something he must give you before telling you *what to do,* and that is an awareness of *who you are.* Is somebody giving you a nasty problem? God must show you who you are to be—his child who reflects his character—before he can show you what you need to do. If your being is right, your doing cannot possibly go wrong. Only when that priority fully prevails are you headed for what God would call success, and his successes are the only real ones.

5
Pecksniffian Praying

Mr. Pecksniff said grace: a short and pious grace, invoking a bless-
ing on the appetites of those present, and committing all persons
who had nothing to eat to the care of Providence, whose business
(so said the grace, in effect) it clearly was, to look after them.
Charles Dickens

IN THIS BOOK I HAVE committed myself in good faith to the
thesis that all prayers are answered, no matter how childish,
how selfish, even how wicked they are, and I believe it. In this
chapter we must consider a kind of praying that puts the
credibility of my thesis to a sore test. I have in mind the
"praying" that results in Pecksniffian prayers moved by painless piety. The prayer of painless piety asks God to do something that will cost the pray-er nothing at all. In Mr. Pecksniff,
Dickens has given us a priceless example of painless piety. If

you haven't read *Martin Chuzzlewit*, I urge you to do so, if for no other reason than the pleasure of meeting this strangely engaging character.

Pecksniff's grace is painless piety on its knees (always provided there is no arthritis in the knees). The Pecksniffian will pray for the hungry as long as it is understood that God, not he, will do the feeding of the hungry.

God within us moves us to pray to God above us; God gives every prayer its initial shove. But the human pray-er is given the responsibility to put into the prayer whatever content he or she chooses. God moves Pecksniff to pray, but not at all in the way that he does.

St. Paul reminds us that it is within our power to grieve the Holy Spirit (Eph 4:30). The Greek word he uses means "to cause pain and distress." We do that to God whenever we act on his impetus to pray but we give no heed to what he teaches us to say to him in prayer. The mind and heart of Christ must supply the content of any prayer if it is to be filial prayer, and no Christian has any right to offer any prayer that is other than that.

Many of us undoubtedly have a problem here. We were given a conventionally Christian upbringing. We were taught as tots that whenever we wanted something we should take it to the Lord in prayer. But we were not taught that before doing so we should consult the Lord himself to ask what he wants us to want. If we were taught in that "good old-fashioned way" to pray for whatever we want, with no question in our mind as to the acceptability of our desire to the Lord, we can go through a long and respectable life without giving a single serious thought to our responsibility in prayer. We may vaguely feel that if God doesn't like what we ask of him, or how we ask, he can disregard it, but meanwhile there's no harm in "running it past" him. Old Pecksniff asks God to feed the hungry, but he adroitly omits to say anything like what Isaiah said: "Here am I: send me!" or what Saul of Tarsus said: "Lord, what do you want me to do?"

We are right in supposing that when we pray, we ask God to do what we cannot do. There is nothing wrong with that basic premise. But we are wrong if we suppose that God asks no more of us than our asking. There is a sound theological truth in C. S. Lewis's statement: "He seems to do nothing of Himself that He can possibly delegate to His creatures."[1] It has everything to do with our praying.

In one of his earlier books Leslie Weatherhead told about a little girl who had a good grip on this truth. She was troubled by the fact that her brother was setting traps for rabbits, and one evening her mother heard her praying aloud, "Dear Lord, please don't let the poor rabbits get caught in Tommy's traps. Don't let them. They can't. They won't. Amen." Her mother, overcome with curiosity, asked, "Darling, how can you be so sure that God will answer your prayer and the rabbits won't be caught?" The child replied with serene confidence, "Because I've already done what God wanted me to do. I jumped on the traps and sprung them!" A delightful story, yes, but she did understand, as God's creature, that God had delegated a part of his own work to her. All of us need that understanding, and above all when we pray.

For many years in the recent past, at every Mass the Roman Catholic Church prayed for the conversion of communist Russia to Christ. And it is true that some members of that Church have offered themselves to God as his agents by going on dangerous missions of evangelism into the Soviet Union. But the mass of the faithful were content to ask God to do something that they wanted to see done—but with no pain or cost to themselves, only the joining in the prayer. Such "praying" takes place in practically every Christian congregation on every Sunday morning. Pecksniffian praying is truly interdenominational, even ecumenical.

There is no gospel in such praying, just sanctimonious hurdy-gurdy. We are not taught by Jesus or by any of his apostles and evangelists that God ever does anything *for* us if we are unwilling for him to do it *through* us. If we join in such painless praying in church, or we engage in it privately, we are not very different, after all, from Mr. Pecksniff. In one respect we come off the worse in the comparison: he is fictitious, thank God; we, alas, are not.

6
Evasive Praying

It is much easier to pray for a bore than to go and see him.
C. S. Lewis

WHAT WE HAVE CALLED Pecksniffian praying is a sanctimonious evasion of duty in which we in effect ask God to run
our errands for us. Closely akin to that artful dodge, yet dis-
tinct from it, is our common practice of letting prayer for
another person become for us our sole duty, the fulfillment
of our obligation. It says, "When I've prayed for Joe or Jane
or for the unemployed or for the heathen in their blindness,
I've done everything that God can possibly require of me.
What more can you do for anybody than to pray?" How easy
to say, "I'll remember you in my prayers!" And indeed how
easy it is to do that, and only that, just to "remember" somebody, to mention him or her to God, perhaps calling God's

attention to that person's need, and to say to our soul: "mission accomplished!"

The black abolitionist Frederick Douglass reported at the end of his career as a lecturer in the cause of emancipation that one of his problems throughout the North was that of finding public auditoriums for his lectures. The best halls available then were churches, so he frequently approached boards of deacons or trustees to ask permission to hold abolitionist meetings in their churches. But whenever their response was "We'll pray about this," their final answer was almost always no. Being conscientious men they probably did the predecision praying, as promised. But because the issue was a controversial one and an affirmative response might have cost their church some members and some contributions, prayer was an attractive and painless way out. It cost them nothing, it took them off the hook, and yet it was a seemingly pious and admirable act.

Can we rightfully call a prayer for somebody else an act of charity when it costs us nothing? Can we call any prayer Christian if it is not an act of charity? Am I being charitable toward that querulous old woman in the rest home for whom I pray *instead of* visiting? It is a terribly easy evasion to fall into. If God is capable of disgust, he must be disgusted with us when we prostitute prayer to any such end.

Earlier I said, in a certain context, that all prayer is good, and in that context the statement is true: everybody, everything prays, and that in itself is good. But in the present context it has to be said that what we may call prayer, and try to pass off as prayer, is in fact sinful if it lacks the character of active charity. "Out of the same mouth proceedeth blessing and cursing," says St. James (3:10). If words from our mouth can either bless or damn, the words we speak to God will have the same effect. Our prayers may be introduced in evidence against us in the Last Judgment.

God has presented us with some human need, and by his very presenting it has commissioned us to get lovingly and helpfully involved in meeting the need, whatever it is. If we use prayer as a substitute for self-involvement, we disobey him. We also add sacrilege to our disobedience by deceptively using a sacred function to disguise our disobedience! What we are talking about here must not be confused with praying while we are going about our duty. That is something entirely different. While we are at work obeying God, doing the task he has presented to us, we must pray for all the grace we need to do the job as God wants it done. What is wrong is substituting prayer for obedience, not prayer for grace and strength to obey.

Some wise Christian whose name is unknown to me has said: "When praying, do not give instructions—report for duty!" It is the best of counsel. If to us God is *Abba,* and if for us prayer is filial, this is our approach: never to pray for anybody without asking God what he wants us to do as he answers our prayer.

But will he always give us something to do that is within our means or power? What if he moves us to pray, let us say, for the conversion to Christ of the Soviet leaders and their nation? What could you or I possibly do, as an action, that could be in any way a part of an answer to that prayer?

It is a good test question, but I think that in our formulation of it we have overlooked something. Action is not always, or only, physical action. Before we can act rightly toward the Soviets, or anyone else, we must learn to think rightly about them. Perhaps we have thought about the leaders in the Kremlin and their subjects as somehow inhuman, or subhuman, or superhuman, but not human in the way that we are. If so, our present attitude needs to be changed, for it is false, ignorant and harmful.

When God has changed somebody's attitude toward somebody else, whether next door or as far away as Moscow from Des Moines, and he has changed it toward the sanity and charity which characterize the mind of Christ in whomever it is found, that is a part of God's answer to the prayer. It is the first and most indispensable part. There can be no change for the better in human relationships until the most basic and entrenched attitudes are changed for the better.

We shall never see the whole, final answer to any prayer until the End, when the secrets of all hearts shall be disclosed and the final results of all our prayers shall be revealed. For the present, we need to understand that God will never move us to pray for anybody or for any purpose unless he sees us as agents he can helpfully use toward the fulfillment of the prayer. What God asks us to provide from our side is a willingness to serve. What he will provide from his side is guidance to our task and the grace to do it well.

7
Magical Praying

*God is not a cosmic bellboy for whom we can press a button
to get things.*
Harry Emerson Fosdick

Pᴇᴄᴋsɴɪғғɪᴀɴ ᴘʀᴀʏɪɴɢ, evasive praying and magical praying are closely akin, yet they can be distinguished. By magic in prayer we mean an assumption that by means of prayer one can manipulate God. That assumption is seldom explicated by anybody today, but it is banefully and widely implicit in much praying. It always has been, and one dreads to think that it always will be. But it is far from extinct. The idea of "prayer power" is pure theological magic.

Jesus is quoted by Matthew as saying: "And all things, whatsoever ye shall ask in prayer, believing, ye shall receive" (Mt 21:22). I have a mental file labeled "Things I wish Jesus never had said," and that file is the repository of this verse. It is one that some people embrace with delight when they want to claim gospel warrant for their magical praying. As they interpret it, this verse gives ample support to a kind of psychic magic which brings you exactly what you want from God—on your terms rather than his. It consists of simply, and absolutely, believing that you are getting what you ask for. Isn't that what the sacred text says?

I wish somebody could explain to me how anybody can believe such nonsense. If it is true, and you want a Cadillac, want it hard enough, ask God for it, and believe that it is arriving in your driveway even as you pray, you will find when you look out your window that there it is, and the wonder-working power of prayer will have done it again!

That may strike you as a parody of an interpretation of a text which I happen to interpret differently. But it isn't. All I have done is to take a widespread understanding of that text and apply it to cases. We hear many people, and they are not all fools, declare that if you have enough faith—by which they mean an expectant fixation so intense that even God could not resist it if he tried—you can get straight from heaven anything you ask for. *Anything*. But you must have faith that is *strong* enough. When these believers in prayer power are asked to explain somebody's failure to make it work, the answer is always the same: his or her faith wasn't strong enough.

Yet, there is that promise of Jesus in the Gospel. How do we explain it without explaining it away?

G. K. Chesterton's comments on Jesus' literary style provide us some help:

Christ had a literary style all his own, not to be found, I think, elsewhere; it consists of an almost furious use of the *a fortiori.* His "how much more" is piled one upon another like castle upon castle in the clouds. The diction *about* Jesus has been, and perhaps wisely, sweet and submissive. But the diction used by Christ himself is quite curiously gigantesque; it is full of camels leaping through needles and mountains hurled into the sea. Morally it is equally terrific; he called himself a sword of slaughter, and told men to buy swords if they sold their coats for them. That he used even wilder words on the side of non-resistance greatly increases the mystery; but it also, if anything, rather increases the violence. We cannot even explain it by calling such a being insane; for insanity is usually along one consistent channel. The maniac is usually a monomaniac. Here we must remember the difficult definition of Christianity as a superhuman paradox whereby two opposite passions may blaze beside each other. The one explanation of the Gospel language that does explain it is that it is the survey of one who from some supernatural height beholds some more startling synthesis.[1]

If we stood on that supernatural height with Jesus, we should, I think, understand everything that he ever said. And unless and until by his grace we stand at last on that height with him, we shall never fully understand anything that he ever said.

So Jesus said something that comes to us as, "Whatever you ask in prayer, believing, you shall receive." The essential truth of this is that there is no limit to what God can do or may do with our prayers, and therefore we need never refrain from asking anything of God simply because we cannot believe that even God can give it. It is another way of saying that with God all things are possible but that belief, trust, faith on our part is indispensable to availing prayer. "He that cometh to God must believe that he is, and that he is a rewarder of them that diligently seek him" (Heb 11:6).

As for moving mountains as obstacles that stand in our way, if God sees that such mountains are real obstructions in the way that he would have us go, he may indeed remove them. I have in mind such mountains as ignorance, prejudice, lack of opportunity, our sins and those of others. There is a faith that moves mountains, that is, a faith through which God moves mountains, and if we don't have it, we must pray for it if we want those mountains moved. However, we must never lose sight of the fact that it is God, not we, who moves the mountains. Another fact to keep always in mind is that when God sees us confronted by mountains, he may give us the strength to surmount and conquer them rather than removing them from us. This is what Theodore Roosevelt had in mind when he said that we should pray not for lighter burdens but for stronger backs.

The right function of faith, in prayer and in life, is to open us up to God and to deliver us over to God. Faith is assurance that God knows perfectly what he is doing and what is best for us. We cannot have faith in God if we have any of that same faith in our own selves. This is a hard saying for many, I know, but if it troubles you think about how we have just defined faith. (You are as entitled to your definition of faith as I am to mine, of course, but if you think there can be such a thing as "faith in one's self," you will have a hard time finding any support for it in the Bible or in historic Christian theology.) Only the humble soul can pray in faith.

The French theologian Alexandre Vinet gave us this definition: "Faith does not consist in the belief that we are saved; it consists in the belief that we are loved."[2] We may ask of God anything that our heart desires, knowing that we are being heard by One who loves us more than we love ourselves and who has all power with which to exercise his love. Those who would want to wheedle, coax or coerce him who is "the King eternal, immortal, invisible, the only wise God" into answering the prayer of a fool according to his folly need to learn the truth about God, about prayer, and about their own selves before they can pray aright. All mistakes about prayer are mistakes about God. Indeed, all mistakes about anything are mistakes about God, because he is Truth, and nothing can be true except as it comes from him and reflects and expresses him.

8
Experience, Not Experiment

I would have no desire other than to accomplish thy will. Teach me to pray; pray thyself in me.
François Fénelon

Boswell reports to us of Dr. Johnson: "He observed that to reason too philosophically on the nature of prayer was very unprofitable."[1] He did not mean that we can overuse our reason on the subject of prayer. Being a truly wise man, he knew that we cannot do that on any subject. But we can use our reason to the exclusion of all other means of obtaining knowledge. Nothing is more unreasonable than the effort to be exclusively cerebral about anything that pertains to the mystery of God or even to the mystery of human life. Those persons whose pretended knowledge of God or humanity rests entirely on what they see with their observing minds can know nothing at all of either mystery.

Johnson was a contemporary of Voltaire and Hume. When skeptical thinkers of that age thought about such things as prayer and miracles, they thought philosophically, asking such questions as this: "Is it reasonable to suppose that a God who rules his universe by laws would set aside any of those laws to accommodate the whim of some puny creature who prays for it?" Today skeptics or unbelievers are more likely to resort to what they call the scientific method—a method of inquiry which has wrought wonders incredible and innumerable in the physical sciences but has accomplished nothing whatever in those so-called human sciences which are neither quite human nor quite scientific.

A cardinal dogma of the modern rationalist is that if the truth of a proposition cannot be verified by scientifically controlled experimentation, it cannot in reason be accepted as true. How then does one go about learning whether God answers prayer? On the rationalistic principle one could do this by using one hundred cancer patients, presumed to be terminally ill, as guinea pigs, with a team of research assistants praying for the healing of fifty of them and leaving the other fifty unprayed for. The results would be accepted as evidential grounds for an answer to the question about the efficacy of prayer.

What's wrong with such a project? Everything, to a Christian mind. The idea of it is both preposterous and blasphemous. How could any lover of God and of human beings pray for some people in dire need of help, but withhold prayer from others in the same need, purely in the interest of making a point in a debate? I know that some comparisons are odious indeed, but when I think about this mentality, the Nazi scientists whose guinea pigs were human beings come instantly to mind. They too were dispassionate researchers, "pure scientists." I thank God that all scientific researchers I know, or know about, are not dispassionate researchers and "pure scientists."

Nobody who knows God as *Abba* could dream of suggesting to him that this is his golden opportunity to collaborate in an experiment that could well turn out to be "the story of the year" in both the scientific and religious worlds. Lest we forget—"God is not mocked" (Gal 6:7).

Prayer is an experience, not an experiment, and God does not respond to our stimuli in the manner of a well-behaved laboratory rat.

Many years ago a famous Hollywood actress wrote a book entitled *Why Not Try God?*[2] Long before I came to a man's estate or to any serious interest in theology, it seemed to me that the title itself was a blasphemy, that if God exists at all it is not for us to try him but for him to try us.

H. G. Wells wrote a telling parable about this in the form of a story. It was about a modern and modernistic archbishop who hadn't really prayed for years, if ever, but was constantly exhorting troubled ladies to "try prayer, my dear, try prayer." He was a cheery soul, and for a long time his life was blissfully untroubled. But one day things began to go wrong, gradually but unremittingly. His self-confidence dried up completely until he decided to try God and try prayer as he had so freely counseled others. Certainly it could do no harm to try. The story continues:

Yes, he would pray.

Slowly he sank to his knees and put his hands together. He was touched by a kind of childish trustfulness in his own attitude. "O God," he began, and paused.

He paused, and a sense of awful imminence, a monstrous awe, gripped him. And then he heard a voice.

It was not a harsh voice, but it was a strong, clear voice. There was nothing about it still or small.

"Yes," said the voice. "What is it?"

They found His Grace in the morning. He had slipped off the steps on which he had been kneeling, and lay sprawling on the crimson carpet. Plainly his death had been instantaneous.

But instead of the serenity, the almost fatuous serenity, that was his habitual expression, his countenance, by some strange freak of nature, displayed an extremity of terror and dismay.[3]

It would have been better for the poor man if occasionally during his halcyon years he had pondered such texts as this: "It is a fearful thing to fall into the hands of the living God" (Heb 10:31). But no less is it a joyful thing to put ourselves in love and trust into those hands; and that is what filial prayer seeks to do, and does.

Christians have a unique self-awareness of who they are vis-à-vis God. This is not to say that they are dearer to God than others, or even that their prayers are "processed" more expeditiously; God may well be happier with many prayers he receives from some non-Christians than with some from pillars of the church. But all other *theophiloi*, friends of God, are *seekers* of him. They "seek the Lord, if haply they might feel after him, and find him, though he be not far from every one of us" (Acts 17:27). Christians, on the other hand, know themselves as *found* by God. Christ is God finding them. So when they pray they seek God only in the way that children seek their father or mother when in need or when hungering for their presence, not as searchers for God who know not where, how, or if they will find him. This self-awareness profoundly determines the spirit and content of all authentically Christian praying.

If our knowledge of God is the knowledge which Jesus imparts, we have no desire to receive from him anything other than what he chooses to give, because we know that what we ask can only be inferior to what he gives. And so our prayers become not at all an asking God for what we want in the manner of a child telling his dad what he wants for Christmas. They become reviewing our wants and desires in our Father's presence. He already knows perfectly what we want, but our spelling it all out with him gives him a chance to show us what we *really* want if we want the best.

Countless times I have been shown the selfishness or wrongness of something I wanted when I spelled it out to him and to myself, both together. So years ago I gave up almost entirely saying to God "Please give me" and began saying in effect: "Lord, you know what I want. I want it very badly; there's no use pretending that I don't. But I won't be disappointed if you say no. I know that what you give will be the best, and I hope you will make me realize that it is truly so, to my heart's full content." In one way or another, at once or later, I am given that realization, with contentment and peace.

I am not saying that my way of "letting my requests be made known to God" is better than any other. But if it isn't better than the "please give me" approach, I must conclude that my own experience in two-way communication with God has been either totally deceptive or totally unique—neither of which I can believe.

9
Prayer and Miracle

Whatever a man prays for, he prays for a miracle. Every prayer reduces itself to this: Great God, grant that two twice two be not four.
Ivan Sergeyevich Turgenev

THERE IS AN ODD MIX of sense and nonsense in Turgenev's statement that every prayer asks of God that "twice two be not four."[1] Every prayer does not reduce itself to what he says it does. You and I and millions of others regularly pray for no such thing as that two times two may not equal four. I, for one, practically live by the prayer that God will keep firmly fixed, as it now is, the order of things exemplified by two times two equals four. If ever that comes unstuck, I don't want to be around. When occasionally somebody comes along with a bright theory that our old arithmetic is no good and he has a better one to offer, or any similar theory in physics or morality or art that would abolish some basic stabilizing sanctity, I pray that he may be found wrong.

What Turgenev says about every prayer being for a miracle is right, though what he means by a miracle and what some others of us mean are two quite different things. He thinks it would be a miracle if God granted the prayer that two times two should no longer equal four. I think it would be terrible, but also no longer a miracle: it would be rather an abdication by the Almighty of his throne of power.

A miracle is not necessarily a violation or reversal or suspension of any law of God's ordered world, although when we speak of the "laws of nature" we must keep in mind that they are God's laws, not nature's, and he may, and surely will, execute and administer them as he wills. *Nothing* takes place simply because such "laws of nature" as the law of gravity necessitate it. A law has no power of its own to act; it must be activated and applied by a will with executive power. *Anything* that takes place does so because God says to it, "Take place!" It is as Chesterton somewhere remarked: The sun does not rise in the morning because the earth spins on its axis; it rises because God says to it, "Get up!" Behind any "law of nature" is the mind, will and purpose of God. The divine will is always free, never bound by what may appear *to our limited vision* as restrictions not only on our freedom of action but on God's. When in the End we are given to see how God governs his creation, we shall see, I am sure, how God performs his wonders without breaking or even bending his own laws.

The word *miracle* explains itself if we let it. A *miraculum* is a wonderful work of God, and all his works are wonderful, each in its own way. If we ask God for anything, when we see it as it is we can only wonder at it, and that makes it a miracle.

It is as Walt Whitman says: "A mouse is miracle enough to stagger sextillions of miracles."[2] Any gift of God's love is a miracle, and in a true vision and appreciation of it we can only be "lost in wonder, love, and praise."[3] You pray, telling God what you think you want for yourself or for somebody else, and he gives you either what you ask for or something better (most of the time, in my experience at least, the latter). That is the miracle you pray for and you unfailingly get.

What, then, can be said about our common propensity, and common it is, for asking that two times two may come to something other than four, or something equally anarchic, so that "just this once" God might accommodate himself to what we consider our special need at the moment? If there is any trace of such special-interest pleading in our prayer, it can only be because we have not been listening to the Voice within us that speaks through what we call our common sense. (About this, of course, Emerson may be right when he says that "common sense is as rare as genius.")[4]

We all take for granted that we are well endowed with common sense even though we may have no other intellectual gift. If we try to be sane when we pray, we should find it within our power to eliminate from our praying the nonsense of which Turgenev accuses us, if for no other reason than that the *last* thing we want is that all of a sudden, because we or some other rash fool requested it, the "God of Things As They Are" would become the "God of Things As They Are Now until Further Notice, but Didn't Used to Be."

Users of the *Book of Common Prayer* in their worship are accustomed to thank God for "our creation, preservation, and all the blessings of this life."[5] Once God has created us, he must continue creating us toward the end he has in view for us; and in order to preserve us through our continuing creation, he must protect us from simply spinning off into nowhere and nothingness by providing for us a secure order in which to grow. It must be a secure order in its physical, mental and moral dimensions.

Because that is so, whenever we feel any impulse to ask God to do anything for us which could be granted only by weakening or destroying some rampart that protects us, we may please him by canceling our order before we place it. Jean Ingelow once said, "I have lived to thank God that my prayers have not all been answered." Well may we all say that not all our prayers have been answered, at least not in the way we hoped when we offered them. But it would be better to consider, before we pray, whether what we have in mind to ask makes good sense.

Few prayers have appealed to so many people, and for good reason, as Reinhold Niebuhr's Serenity Prayer, as it is commonly called: "God, give us grace to accept with serenity the things that cannot be changed, courage to change the things which should be changed, and the wisdom to distinguish the one from the other." We all need all we can get of that wisdom to distinguish between what we may responsibly ask of God and what we may not.

Prayer for that wisdom should always be part of our preparation and approach to prayer. Few things can please our Father more surely than our earnest effort to get our brains together before we pray, so that we can talk our best sense in our conversation with him. What is the first and great commandment? "Thou shalt love the Lord thy God with all thy heart, and with all thy soul, and with all thy *mind*" (Mt 22:37). This does not mean that the more intellectual we are, the better we can pray. Mind is not intellect. A person with a low IQ using his mind when he prays is better prepared (will make more sense to God) than will any intellectual who does not use his mind. God says to each one of us what he said to sulking Jonah: "Just think, man, think, before you tell me what you think I ought to do!"

We need never refrain from asking anything of God simply on the ground that we think it impossible. God specializes in "impossible" things that are too good to be true. What we need to do is to think before we pray and while we are praying, about what, to the best of our knowledge, God might be able to grant of our requests without tearing his—and our—whole world apart.

Coleridge once remarked that "prayer is the effort to live in the spirit of the whole."[6] He meant the effort to see everything, as best we can, as God must see it. I cannot doubt that whenever we make that effort God joyfully responds by enlarging our vision of the whole. When we pray in that spirit, we expect miracles and we get them—miracles as rightly understood—and we refrain from asking God to discombobulate his whole universe so that our two times two might turn out, for once, to come to 3.1416, or whatever other crazy thing we happen to want at the moment.

10
Answer or Autosuggestion?

The Beyond is the Within.
Author unknown

WHEN GOD ANSWERS PRAYERS, or we think he does, is it really God who answers or we who answer ourselves? The unbeliever holds that all prayer is simply a talking with ourselves, like a child carrying on an imaginary conversation through a toy telephone. He holds that when we ask God to give us peace of mind, and we get peace of mind, it is really a successful autosuggestion rather than a gift from heaven.

This is one of those arguments which you may not accept as valid but which you may find difficult if not impossible to refute. You can turn the debate into a stalemate by challenging your opponent to prove that the gift is from you to yourself rather than from God to you. But you will be as stymied as he is if he challenges you to prove the contrary. In fact, such a stalemate settles nothing.

The issue is one which cannot be settled on strictly and exclusively rational grounds. It is a matter of faith for either believer or unbeliever. The atheist must have faith in the non-being of God no less than the believer's faith in God's being. This fact may explain why there are so few real atheists: there simply isn't enough of their kind of faith to go around.

I approach the question this chapter deals with as a believer, and I have no intention of trying to prove, or disprove, anything. I will say only that the belief that the Person on "the other end of the line" when we pray is God rather than our own selves makes sense to me, and the alternative—that what we call prayer is simply autosuggestion—does not.

In her book *To Pray and to Grow,* Flora Slosson Wuellner writes:

We know there is no such thing as unanswered prayer. But the answers are usually unexpected and sometimes surprising. So we must keep alert and aware of answers coming to us along unorthodox channels. We can be very practical and down to earth about this. We can commit to God the difficult letter we have to write, and new ideas start forming. We can mentally turn over to Him a quarrelsome committee and hold each separate member in His light during the meeting. Watch what happens! We can approach a counseling session not knowing what to say, or sit down to write a sermon, or a book, or a speech, and find ideas forming that we didn't even know we had. We can commit to Him the antipathy we feel toward someone and find new unexpected depths of compassion opening in us. We can give Him any pain, any problem, any closed door or dead end

in our lives. He will take it. And something will happen.[1]
Such has been my own experience, so regularly that it would
be insane to question it, and so of course I think it is all
answered prayer rather than autosuggestion.

Consider, for example, what happens when we "commit to
God the difficult letter we have to write, and new ideas start
forming." The skeptic may point out that what we call "committing to God the task confronting us" usually involves some
serious advance consideration of that task, and that this may
well explain the new ideas that start forming. In short, God
had nothing to do with it, but our mental activity did.

I answer that the mental activity was God's answer to our
prayer—an answer actually given before we prayed and during
our praying. Theologians speak of "prevenient grace," meaning divine grace which God gives us before we need it to
enable us to desire to do what we ought. There is no reason
why we should not expect that God's answers to our prayers
should not be prevenient—given to us before we even ask.
After all, he knows what we are going to ask, and he knows
what we need and what he intends to give, all in advance of
our needing and our asking and his giving.

If God answers any prayer of the sort we are now thinking
about, he may well do so through our mental activity because
it is from that activity that the good ideas have to emerge. He
who creates all our organs and faculties knows which one he
needs to use for any particular blessing. If he chooses to give
us healing from sickness, it will be through our bodily or-
ganism, of course. But that is not to say that the healing comes
from our own bodies rather than from him.

We mentally turn over to God a quarrelsome committee
and hold each separate member in God's light during the

meeting. "Watch what happens!" Well, what does? If nothing else, our act of holding up each separate member to God in prayer changes our relationship to the committee as a whole and to each individual member, for the reason expressed by William Law in these words: "There is nothing that makes us love a man so much as praying for him."[2]

Every word we speak or suggestion we put forward in that meeting will be a fruit of our prayer and will inject into the whole process of the meeting a more loving and harmonious element. The effect may not be discerned or felt by the participants, or on the contrary it may be so overpowering that they all wonder what has come over them and got into them. We never know. And it doesn't greatly matter, if at all, whether we discern or feel God's answers to prayers as long as he gives them.

Why God does not always—if ever—answer our prayer so emphatically, so unmistakably, that there can be no reasonable doubt as to who is doing it and what he is doing, is one of those things that God has never explained. He not only teaches us to pray without ostentation (Mt 6:5-6), he answers prayer in the same manner. Since he does not reveal his mind and purpose in this matter, we can only surmise. But as a Christian I do this with some confidence.

The Father reveals himself to us in his Son, and while his Son lived among us in our flesh, he was very reticent about his mighty works. This fact is most conspicuous in St. Mark's account of Christ's ministry, the earliest of the four Gospels. Jesus did not want people to believe in him *because of* his mighty works, but for some other reason entirely. That reason, I submit, is that he wanted people to see and to know and to love God manifest in him—not for what God could do for them, but for God himself, the infinitely loving and lovable. The knowledge and love of God as God is in himself is its own reward. The ultimate answer to all prayer is—God himself.

Thus understood, every prayer is answered and every answer is a miracle—a wonder. But it is only as we receive, ponder and lovingly cherish each of these miracles in our own heart, inwardly, silently, intimately between God and ourselves, that we grow in the knowledge and love of him. An answer to prayer which shines wonderfully to the outward eye may be granted, and it may increase the faith of the beholders. But an answer to our prayer which is received not through outward sense but through the inward vision of the heart increases not only our faith but our love and knowledge of him who answers. It has the effect of making us love God not for his works' sake but for himself.

That may not be all or even part of the reason God so often answers our prayers so unspectacularly, but I can't think of a better one.

11
God's Problem
or Ours?

You're either part of the solution or part of the problem.
Eldridge Cleaver

WHEN CLEAVER SAID THAT we are either part of the solution or part of the problem, he was referring to the problem of race relations in America, and he was right. But what he said is applicable to every problem, personal or social, that we can face. Moreover, we have no problems that are ours ultimately. They are all God's, but to him they are not what we commonly mean by the word. To us a problem is a difficulty that we have to face and to solve as best we can, and if we can. Every real problem seems like that to us on our side, but not to God on his side. The problem is his, and he knows what he will do with it, and he never fails.

There are two possible approaches to God about "our"

problems (which are ours only to the extent that we are directly involved in them). Between these two approaches lies the difference between the fulfillment and nonfulfillment of that *realized working union with God* which is the proper human end of all prayer.

In one approach we say, "Lord, I've got this problem. Please help me to solve it." This seems a humble and realistic approach, but it is wrong insofar as it implies that God is there to help us with our projects rather than to use us in his projects. In the other approach we say, "Lord, here is this problem, and I can't handle it, but I know you can and will. Because I'm personally involved in it, I know that you want to use me in working it out; so show me what you want me to do, and give me the grace and wisdom and resolution I need to do it."

God is in complete command of everything that goes on in this world. He has created us to be his partners in time, it is true, and when we err in judgment or flout God's will, we do in some sense create a "problem" for him. But he need not face his problems with perplexity and self-doubt as we face ours. He knows what to do, that he can do it, and that he will. However, he gives to us who have been "part of the problem" a chance to be "part of the solution." And when we, facing the problem from our side, ask God for his help, we do so as his children who are also his servants, agents, junior partners reporting for duty.

What is to us a problem is to God simply a complication in some divine project in his continuing creation of his world. William James offers this apt parable:

> Suppose two men before a chess-board—the one a novice, the other an expert player of the game. The expert intends

to beat. But he cannot foresee what any actual move of his adversary may be. He knows however all the *possible* moves of the latter; and he knows in advance how to meet each of them by a move of his own which leads in the direction of victory. And the victory infallibly arrives, after no matter how devious a course, in the one predestined form of check-mate to the novice's king.[1]

God is not exactly like the expert chess player. He is not like any of his creatures—not even "experts." It cannot be said of God that he "cannot foresee what any actual move of his adversary may be," for he has complete foreknowledge. But in the parable the chess player controls the game: it is *his* game because he is complete master of it, in a way that at least hints at the way in which God controls his game of completing the world.

The classic example in the Bible of how God plays his game is told in Genesis in the story of Joseph and his brethren. What the envious brothers do to young Joseph is clearly contrary to God's will. They are fallen, sinful men, like us, and therefore free to make countermoves against God as his adversaries, and that they do. But because Joseph is wickedly sold into Egypt, God has him in the right place to accomplish, through him, the deliverance of his people from death by famine. In the great disclosure scene when Joseph reveals himself to his brothers, he shows himself to be not only magnanimous but theologically perceptive: "Be not grieved, nor angry with yourselves, that ye sold me hither: for God did send me before you to preserve life" (Gen 45:5). What Joseph's brothers did was not a good move. No sin ever brings any profit to anybody. God, however, "the Master of the Show," can always checkmate the adversary's king—can use the very complication resulting from our sin or folly to accomplish his perfect end. Thus, always "the fierceness of man shall turn to [God's] praise" (Ps 76:10).[2]

What I have been saying is not to suggest that all problems are the results of somebody's sin or folly, but simply that they are all ultimately *God's* business rather than our own. It is for him to solve them and for us to serve him as he does so. Suppose that somebody dear to you is in great trouble. Your heart longs to help, but you don't know how you can. So you pray. If you pray with right understanding, you know that the work to be done is God's. Yet you do not say "Over to you, Lord—you take it from here!" In the spirit of Isaiah you say, "Here am I: send me" (Is 6:8).

As that becomes our fixed attitude and regular practice, we learn by experience how wonderful, wise and *mighty* is the Love that answers our prayers and the Power that solves what we call "our" problems. Yet one caveat is needed here. Sometimes after we have prayed and have done our part we are given to see a quick and happy issue.

God answers sharp and sudden on some prayers,

And thrusts the thing we have prayed for in our face.[3]

In such a case we may happily consider the whole case to be closed: we've done our part, God has done his, and so we can turn to the next problem, he and we together.

But there are other cases that do not turn out so speedily and happily. We pray, we do what God gives us to do, and the problem remains unsolved and possibly worse. Why doesn't God do better with it? Or is it we who have failed?

This anxiety is human—and erroneous. What we fail to see is that *nothing* is *ever* finished in this present world—not even those cases we considered so happily closed. No case is ever closed in God's file, marked either unsolved or completed. Only in heaven is any case finally closed. In the end we shall see how perfect was the solution—"the grand Amen"—of each problem, from its beginning, and indeed from the very foundation of the world. "Only God can finish," as Ruskin said, and he always does.

12
Answers in Installments

You must distinguish between delays and denials.
Thomas Brooks

RECENTLY IN HIS DAILY COLUMN Dr. Billy Graham responded to a reader's question about answers to prayer, and he said that God's answer to any prayer is either *yes, no* or *wait*. That is a good rough-and-ready reply, but I think it needs further honing. What we ordinarily consider a *yes* reply to prayer is in fact only the first installment of an answer that God will be giving eternally. When we get what we consider a *no* answer, we are wrong if we take it as final. *Any* answer we get at the moment we pray, or soon after, or any time before we die, is in fact still a *wait* answer. We are asked to wait until we see the final end of the matter. We must always wait for that as long as we are in time and space, because the final answer is eternal.

There is a true story which to my mind perfectly illuminates the meaning of what we conventionally consider a *no* from God. If we knew nothing more than this incident in the life of Thomas Carlyle, we should know from it that he was a man who knew how to hear God in his soul.

Carlyle had spent ten years, days of toil and nights of waking, preparing the manuscript of *The French Revolution*. During those years he and his wife were very poor. After he had finished the immense task, writing it all on foolscap and making no copy, he took the manuscript to his friend John Stuart Mill who had promised to give it a thoroughly critical reading. Mill placed the enormous bundle of paper on a mantel, intending to begin reading it the next day. But when he came to get it, he saw that it was gone. A housemaid had thought it was scrap paper and had lit a fire with it. Ten years of toil and trouble had gone up in smoke.

With heavy heart Mill had to go to Carlyle's home to tell him what had happened. After he had done so and left, Carlyle reported the catastrophe to his wife and mentioned how pale and shaken Mill had been about it. That night he recorded it in his diary and added: "It was as if my Invisible Schoolmaster had torn up my copy book when I showed it to him and had said, 'No, boy, thou must write it better!' " The next day he went to work writing it better.

Whenever we get a *no* answer from God, he is trying to tell us something that we need to know. This applies to all our prayers and all our undertakings. In Carlyle's case God was clearly saying, "You must write it better." Carlyle, remember, was a Christian who knew that God's will must prevail in all things, and that nothing contrary to God's will ought to satisfy us. When we fail in some enterprise it is God saying *no*. He may want to say to us, "You must try again, and do better next time." Or he may want us to do something else altogether. We make it possible for us to hear what he is saying when we put our minds to work thoroughly examining the attendant facts and circumstances of our situation and we ask God to show us what steps he wants to take as we go along. So doing, we make ourselves guidable to him. And when we do this, we eventually come to a point at which we look back upon that *no* God spoke to us and we see it as it really was— another manifestation of God's loving providence and caring.

One of the inestimable advantages of having a mind steeped in the Bible is that God will often give us the guidance we need through some Scripture. But he speaks to us through *all* our experiences, without exception. God's hand is directly at work in everything that "happens." I put "happens" in quotes to suggest that there is no event that "just happens" as though it were not a part of God's Master Plan. A happening, if one ever "happened," would be entirely pointless and purposeless. There really are no accidents if by an accident we mean a happening without cause. Isaac Bashevis Singer wisely suggests that "the word 'accident' should be erased from the dictionary."[1]

But with the case of Carlyle's manuscript in mind, you may want to challenge that statement. Wasn't that an accident, a most flagrant and tragic one? Yes, the maid burned the manuscript in her ignorance. Yes, Mill ought to have put the bundle in a safe place. But these were only secondary causes of what happened. God's good purpose for Thomas Carlyle was the ultimate cause. Carlyle's labor over all those years was really a prayer that his book would be a good one. God did not want a good book from him but a great one, the one he knew his man Thomas was capable of writing.

"There's a divinity that shapes our ends, roughhew them how we will"—and in the course of his doing so, that divinity often says *no* to us.[2] If he did not, he could not shape our ends as he wants them shaped. And if we had anything like a sufficient knowledge of our own eternal best interests, we would want no less.

If God loved us less, he could say *yes,* make us happy at the moment, and let us skip gaily on to a mediocre or bad performance, or to some catastrophe. Some of us are old enough to remember Al Smith, Herbert Hoover's Democratic opponent in the 1928 election. Al was decisively beaten. Undoubtedly he and his supporters prayed for victory, and the answer was an emphatic *no.* But the next year came the Wall Street collapse and the beginning of the Great Depression. The man in the White House had not caused the problem and could not cure it, but he had to take the blame and pay the price politically.

When Al saw what was happening, he remarked, "I feel like the man who just missed the train that went off the open end of the drawbridge!" I don't know whether or not he linked his political fate with his prayers; he was wise if he did. God spared him what poor Hoover had to suffer, by saying *no* to his prayers for victory in the election. (Don't ask me to explain why God answered Hoover's prayers for victory in the way that he did. That is something between God and Herbert Hoover, one of the noble and tragic figures in American history.)

One more point. God answers in installments every prayer offered to him. In a sense it's like the old serial movies that were the delight and frequent terror of the childhood of most of us who grew up in the pre-television era. At the end of each episode we were left dangling in suspense until the next one, a whole interminable week later. Likewise, the answer to *any* prayer is an unfolding mystery in which we must wait till that End in which faith will be lost in sight, suspense lost in relief, disappointment lost in fulfillment and dazed delight as we see how much better the completed answer eternally is than we had ever dreamed of, or thought possible, when we prayed.

13
Prayer
as Attention

Vision is the art of seeing things invisible.
Jonathan Swift

"PRAYER CONSISTS OF ATTENTION. It is the orientation of all the attention of which the soul is capable toward God."[1] Simone Weil's essay in which this statement is found is astonishing for its originality of approach, and if you are as troubled as I am by the difficulty of attentiveness to God, you will find her wisdom enlightening and helpful. I often despair of my ability to fix my attention exclusively on God for two solid minutes. And believing as I do that our whole experience of life is meant to be basic training for that eternal unbroken "attention to God" which will be heaven's delight, this is a mote troubling my mind's eye as I think about my eternal future. I am sure this difficulty of attention is shared by many.

In her essay Weil goes on to discuss school studies and other mental disciplines as aids to prayer. A person may spend a whole year in intense concentration on a mathematical problem without solving it, but the effort itself has strengthened the capacity for sustained attention, and this is superb preparation for prayer. It is also superb preparation for that "attention to God" which is our eternal life: "And this is life eternal, that they might know thee the only true God, and Jesus Christ whom thou hast sent" (Jn 17:3). "Every effort," Weil says, "adds a little gold to a treasure no power on earth can take away. The useless efforts made by the Curé d'Ars, for long and painful years, to learn Latin bore fruit in the marvelous discernment that enabled him to see into the very soul of his penitents behind their words and even their silences."[2]

That is a valuable and happily usable insight. When the simple priest was struggling unsuccessfully to master Latin, he was unwittingly strengthening himself in prayer and spiritual discernment. Here was one of God's delightfully odd answers to prayer, of which he seems to be very fond. A moving testimony to this was found in the pocket of a dead Confederate soldier whose name is unknown. It reads:

I asked for strength that I might achieve;
    He made me weak that I might obey.
I asked for health that I might do greater things.
    I was given grace that I might do better things.
I asked for riches that I might be happy.
    I was given poverty that I might be wise.
I asked for power that I might have the praise of men.
    I was given weakness that I might feel the need of God.
I asked for all things that I might enjoy life.
    I was given life that I might enjoy all things.

I received nothing that I asked for.

All that I hoped for.

My prayer was answered.

This man's attention to God had been developed by disciplined, loving, obedient attention to all the things he had to deal with, and the result was his serenely joyful discovery that God always gives us either what we ask or something better.

Prayer as attention to God needs to be considered not only psychologically, as training and strengthening our wobbly wills, but theologically as a part of our preparation for eternal life. We never come to know God, or anybody else, merely by contemplating him. We come to know him only by sharing life with him. Yet we never come to know anybody without contemplation. Intense and continuing attention to each other is in fact a part of sharing life together.

Imagine two wounded soldiers lying close together on a battlefield, who have been undiscovered and unrescued. They have some water and rations between them. They know they are in imminent peril of death, and they share life in order to survive. They also share reminiscences, confidences, hopes and fears, in mutual attention. Each learns more about the other in an hour than he might otherwise learn in fifty years.

We learn who God is by sharing life with him, and this includes our attention to him as he unceasingly attends to us. By being volunteer agents of his loving, and thus participants in it, we share his life. The cup of cold water given for his sake is an attention to him which enhances our vision, knowledge and love of him.

When I spoke earlier of the (for me at least) great difficulty of attention to God in prayer, I had in mind what we normally mean by prayer: talking to God. We do better to think of prayer as conversation with God, because in all complete prayer we listen as well as talk. We need to grow in conversational attentiveness to God—in our listening (which we discussed earlier, pp. 32-34) as well as our speaking. Then we need also to enlarge our concept of prayer to include two expressions of it: the prayer of words and the prayer of action. For fifteen centuries the great religious order of the Benedictines has had as its motto *Laborare est orare* ("To work is to pray"). They mean work shared with God. The prayer of words is conversation with God; the prayer of work is cooperation with God in his continuing creation of his world.

Both forms of prayer require utmost attention on our part. Attention to God is meditation on his ways and observation of his workings, and as we learn more of his works and ways, we frame our lives accordingly.

We pay more attention to God in our prayer of work by being more diligent in our loving not only in our hearts but with our hands. This helps our attending to him in the prayer of words by giving us more to "talk over" with him. "We know that in everything God works for good with those who love him." This Revised Standard Version's translation of Romans 8:28 is much better than the Authorized Version's, "We know that all things work together for good to them that love God." "Things" do not work together, or at all, by themselves; they have to be worked by somebody. God works for good *with* those who love him.

Perhaps a caveat is needed here. Many Christians find it attractive and inspiring to think of the working relationship between God and us as a *partnership* corresponding to a human partnership, with God as the senior partner and his human helper as the junior. This concept is biblically insupportable and theologically indefensible. We are never indispensable to God. He is in no way or degree dependent on our help. It is out of love for us as his children rather than out of need for us as his helpers that he works with and through us. He is our Father, giving us freedom to grow and to advance in our filial service.

When any two personal beings, divine or human, are working together in shared love for the object of their effort, a unique bond develops between them. If this doesn't give them something to talk about—when they can find time to talk—it's hard to imagine what else can.

Weil is right in saying that anything that develops our power of mental concentration increases our ability to attend to God. But she does not mean, and we must not take her to mean, that the greater our intellectual capacity, the greater our power of attention to God. Attention, the power of concentration, is a matter of the will, not of the mind. Sharing God's work with him as he continues his creation is by far the most effective attention-developer. His most active servants all testify that the more they try to do for him, the more they have to say to him—and he to them.

14
Prayer
and Honesty

Deep down in me I knowed it was a lie, and He knowed it. You can't pray a lie—I found that out.
Huckleberry Finn

Is it possible to be perfectly honest with God when we pray? Is it possible to be perfectly honest with anybody else, or with ourselves? The first step toward honesty is to be honest about our own honesty, to face these questions, to search our souls. We are thinking here about human possibilities. With God all things are possible except that he should deny his own being, which is Truth. That is to say that God is absolutely honest. But is absolute honesty ever possible for us—even in prayer?

Huck said that you can't pray a lie. He had tried it, and the effort blew up in his face. The royal murderer in *Hamlet* cannot pray because he cannot repent and honestly acknowledge his offense:

My words fly up, my thoughts remain below:
Words without thoughts never to heaven go.[1]

We have two questions: whether we can be perfectly honest with God, and whether we can be perfectly honest with anybody else or with ourselves. The second of these is easier to answer, and I'm afraid the answer has to be no. Perfect honesty would be a total absence of self-deception and of desire to deceive others; it would be total integrity.

Orthodox theology teaches that we lost our integrity in the Fall. Integrity consists of being an integer, an undivided and indivisible unit in our own being, with no division within the self. Nobody with rudimentary self-knowledge can fail to see the plurality of selves within himself: "There are three Johns: (1) the real John, known only to his Maker; (2) John's ideal John, never the real one, and often very unlike him; (3) Thomas's ideal John, never the real John, nor John's John, but often very unlike either."[2]

John has convinced himself that his ideal John is the real one, and he automatically tries to impose that fiction on everybody he meets. He does this unconsciously because it has become a conditioned reflex in human life. No animal other than man is capable of such habitual hypocrisy (or, indeed, of any hypocrisy at all—blessed creatures). On all human evidence we must confess that we are unable, by our own effort, to escape or transcend this warp in our woof; we simply cannot be entirely honest with other people or with our own selves. *O Adam, quid fecisti?* ("O Adam, what have you done?")

To our other question: Can we be honest with God—present ourselves to him with no pretenses, no fig leaves? I am not certain that we can, but I am very sure that our only chance of achieving honesty with anybody, or even coming close to it, is when we pray. The reason this is so seems fairly obvious. If God is as believing Jews, Christians, and Muslims believe him to be, it follows that to him "all hearts are open, all desires known, and from [him] no secrets are hid."[3]

Given that premise, anybody would have to be a consummate dummy to suppose that he or she could deceive God. I wish we could all believe without a struggle that there is no dummy so bad off as that in the whole tribe of *homo insipiens;* but having lived full threescore years and ten, I have seen some strange things, and not all of them outside myself.

Such extreme stupidity, however, is almost as rare as genius. Therefore, it is safe to say that when anybody above that lowest level of intelligence prays with any real knowledge that he is presenting himself naked before the all-seeing and all-knowing One, he is much more inclined to be honest than he is with anybody else. He has nothing to lose, since God already knows the whole of him.

O LORD, thou hast searched me, and known me. Thou knowest my downsitting and mine uprising, thou understandest my thought afar off. Thou compassest my path and my lying down, and art acquainted with all my ways. For there is not a word in my tongue, but, lo, O LORD, thou knowest it altogether. . . . My substance was not hid from thee, when I was made in secret, and curiously wrought in the lowest parts of the earth. (Ps 139:1-4, 15)

God has known everything about us, our every thought, word and deed, from the very foundation of the world, so he is quite impossible to deceive. Prayer is self-exposure to him, and some people avoid praying for that very reason. Their good sense tells them what it is, and they don't want it!

A generation ago there was a wonderful old priest, Canon George Gibson, in charge of the Cathedral Shelter in Chicago. He carried on a devoted ministry to derelicts. He had to listen to a constant stream of hard-luck stories, and he always responded with wisdom and compassion, but he also wanted to make certain that every teller of them was telling the truth. When he suspected that somebody was lying, he led the man into the chapel where they prayed together. Sometimes the Canon was moved to pray aloud: "Dear Lord, please help this man to quit being such a damned liar!" The Canon had special reason in such cases for offering that prayer. But it would be in order for every one of us to ask God to help *us* to quit being the "damned liars" that we all are.

Anything less than total honesty is a lie, as John Ruskin well reminds us: "The essence of lying is in deception, not in words; a lie may be told in silence, by equivocation, by the accent on a syllable, by a glance of the eyes attaching peculiar significance to a sentence; and all those kinds of lies are worse and baser by many degrees than a lie plainly worded."[4] Such lying can hardly escape drastic and salutary correction in the praying of a sane person. If we suppose that on the other end of the line is a God who cannot deceive or be deceived, but nevertheless we get down on our knees and try to "con" him, we need psychiatric help—if that can cure us.

Because we know that we cannot deceive God, it is most helpful to present to him our self-deceptions and other-deceptions and to try to blurt out to him what we *really* want, how we *really* feel about anybody or anything. After all, he cannot be surprised or shocked, since we shall be telling him what he already knows. But the simple act of leveling with him is deeply therapeutic. What particular response God will make to any such self-baring we never know, but he will certainly use it to help us quit being liars, to start being more honest with ourselves and others. And honesty is a gift as precious as it is rare.

15
Growing Pains
in Prayer

The Holy Spirit is the loving interiority of God.
Romano Guardini

THERE IS NO SCRIPTURE MORE important to an understanding of Christian prayer than this: "The Spirit helps us in our weakness; for we do not know how to pray as we ought, but the Spirit himself intercedes for us with sighs too deep for words. And he who searches the hearts of men knows what is the mind of the Spirit, because the Spirit intercedes for the saints according to the will of God. We know that in everything God works for good with those who love him, who are called according to his purpose" (Rom 8:26-28 RSV).

We know there is profound truth here, but we are not sure (at least I am not) that we understand each detail in this account of what takes place as the Spirit helps us to pray. I feel that perhaps Paul didn't either, that he was in a position like that of Robert Browning in his later years. When adoring members of the innumerable Browning Clubs would ask the venerated poet what he meant in some obscure passage, he would answer: "Don't ask me! Blest if I know!" That happens to anybody who tries to describe or explain a mystery beyond any mortal's depth.

The Spirit himself intercedes for us with sighs too deep for words. If these were *our* wordless groanings as we wrestle with God, the description would make obvious sense to us, but according to the text they are not our groanings but the Spirit's. About this I will venture boldly. (If we are less than bold about it, we can say nothing positively.) These groanings belong to the Spirit and us *together.* So intimate to us is he that he and we are effectually one spirit, in a way similar to a husband and wife being one flesh (1 Cor 6:17). The travail of prayer makes us groan because such true filial prayer is a new and very demanding experience for us, and our loving Guest and Helper groans with us in the shared agony. (Keep in mind that the word *agony* in its original and basic meaning does not mean excruciating pain but excruciating struggle. *Samson Agonistes* is Samson struggling, not Samson suffering.)

These groanings express our sensation of interior growing pains as we begin, under the Spirit's nurture and tutelage, to make our new home in Christ. It is new to us even if we have been conventionally faithful Christians for eighty years, because it is so radically different from our old life in Adam that we are still having a hard time getting used to it—if in fact we are wanting and trying to get used to it. Prayer in this situation is difficult for us because our pretending to be Christ is being converted into reality. We are being turned into living members of Christ, and the transformation is so painful as well as joyful that our divine Sponsor, the Spirit, groans with us. What this says to us is that the Spirit himself, God in his loving interiority, is completely *with* us, so completely that he feels our growth pains as his own.

He who searches the hearts of men is our Father to whom we pray, and as he receives the Spirit's intercession for us, he understands perfectly: after all, it is God understanding God. Only by human analogy can we imagine what the Spirit says to the Father in these intercessions, but the analogy is found in the perfect humanity of Christ. Even as God the Son prays, "Father forgive them, for they know not what they do," God the Spirit prays, "Father forgive them and hear them, for they know not what to pray."

The Spirit's work is to *Christify* us, to change us within ourselves into conformity with Christ and to incorporate us into Christ. We are the wild olive branches being grafted into the True Vine, and the operation hurts. *The Spirit intercedes for the saints according to the will of God* because God in his three Persons is of one heart, mind and purpose for us.

As we grow into Christ and continue growing in him our praying expresses that growth by becoming more and more a constant communion with God. We are in fact entering into Christ's own communion with the Father, as members of Christ. We are given our best insight to this communion between Father and Son (and thus ourselves as "sons in the Son") in St. John's account of Christ's trial before Pilate (Jn 18:33-37).[1]

In that scene it is clear that Christ is in perfect communion with the Father and that it is Pilate who is being judged. Since God's goal for us is complete conformation to his Son, we know that when the Spirit has finished his work with us our communion with God will be like that which we see in Jesus before Pilate. That life consists of total and unbroken communion with God. When we think about that, and think about ourselves as we now are, we realize that God's goal for us is a long way ahead of us in spiritual distance to be covered.

If we are in Christ, however, we are not appalled or even dismayed by that distance ahead, for we have God himself working for us, with us, within us and through us. The very fact that we find ourselves already at least *pretending* to be Christ when we pray, thinking and praying and trying to live as God's children rather than his mere creatures or tools, means that God has got hold of us and got into us to initiate in us this pretense and then to convert it into reality.

Nobody to my knowledge has described this action of God as well as C. S. Lewis:

An ordinary simple Christian kneels down to say his prayers. He is trying to get into touch with God. But if he is a Christian he knows that what is prompting him to pray is also God: God, so to speak, inside him. But he also knows that all his real knowledge of God comes through Christ, the Man who was God—that Christ is standing beside him, helping him to pray, praying for him. You see what is happening. God is the thing to which he is praying—the goal he is trying to reach. God is also the thing inside him which is pushing him on—the motive power. God is also the road or bridge along which he is being pushed to that goal. So that the whole threefold life of the three-personal Being is actually going on in that ordinary little bedroom where an ordinary man is saying his prayers. The man is being caught up into the higher kind of life . . . being pulled into God,

by God, while still remaining himself.[2]
Remaining himself, yes, but not just as he was before God
started it all—this pulling the pray-er into himself is God's
purpose in moving us to pray. You will remain yourself, you
will never become anybody else, through all eternity. But in
Christ you cannot remain for five minutes just as you were.
God will not allow it. And that's why we must groan as we
grow from creaturely and childish praying into filial and
Christlike praying. It is an agony, a struggle, but there is a
world of difference between the agony of a fight you are
trying to win all by yourself against a terribly fierce and strong
adversary, and the agony of a fight in which the adversary is
even stronger but you have God himself within you, groaning
with you, and you realize that he is, after all, *Almighty* God.

16
The Lord's Prayer Revisited

Jesus teaches us to pray Thy will be done,
not Thy will be changed.
William Barclay

I HAD NOT INTENDED TO WRITE this chapter, but a strange thing happened to me on my way to not writing it. I came upon a book by Hubert van Zeller, *Prayer in Other Words*.[1] In it I find some fresh insights to the Lord's Prayer. So many things have been said by so many people about the Lord's Prayer that I felt we could take our general understanding of it for granted. Reading van Zeller's book has made me see that to write this book without some special consideration of that prayer would be like a performance of *Hamlet* without the Prince. So now we shall briefly run through the familiar (perhaps too familiar) text.

Our Father. Here is a good word from van Zeller: "If it began 'My Father' it might be a more private prayer but it would not have as much charity in it. And charity matters more than privacy."[2]

Who art in heaven. Too seldom are people taught the very important truth that heaven is not some "home beyond the skies" and even beyond our telescopes but is itself the center of all power and dominion over the whole universe. It is both the capital and the powerhouse of the cosmos. All that is, all that happens, is created, ruled, governed from heaven and from nowhere else, and God is the *sole* source and wielder of all power. The power of a Nero or a Stalin or a Hitler is no power at all but rather a protest against the true Power—as feeble as it is false.

Hallowed be thy name. Says van Zeller: " 'Hallowing' means giving glory or worship. The Father's name, our Lord's name, the Holy Spirit's name: it is all one name. You give praise before you start asking for things. God knows well enough what it is that you need, and that in a minute you will be asking for it, but he wants you to begin your prayer on a note of homage. It is like a father telling his son not to snatch."[3] An excellent point, and one commonly neglected. God seeks to "grow us up" into a mature filial relationship with him whenever we pray, and there is no maturity without awareness and appreciation of the Love from whom all blessings flow.

Thy kingdom come. We ought to think hard, and count the cost, before we say this to God, for the reason stated by Aldous Huxley in these words: " 'Our kingdom go' is the necessary and unavoidable corollary of 'Thy kingdom come.' "[4] If that is not what it means for us, it means nothing at all. Van Zeller adds the reminder "that it is a kingdom and not a throne; there are people in it. So there is this notion of all being together in one prayer, under the one king, sharing the one love in charity with others."[5]

Thy will be done, on earth as it is in heaven. "We need not pretend that we are as good at this act of submission as the angels and saints, but at least we can pray that God's will may meet with no resistance. Anyway we mean to accept whatever Providence arranges. Now the more this state of mind is kept up, the more glory we give to God and the holier we become. We take everything in our stride because we know that everything is somehow allowed for in the plan of God. If we can get into that habit of meeting every difficulty, every disappointment, every pleasure and every problem with this clause of the *Our Father* we are in a fair way towards re-living our Lord's life. All the time we shall be echoing his words: 'I came not to do my own will but the will of him who sent me . . . not what I will, but what thou wilt!' "[6]

Give us this day our daily bread. The prayer for the fulfillment of God's will on earth and in our lives precedes our praying for the satisfaction of our wants and needs. God wants us to ask for what we want, but not until we have completely committed our hearts and wills to his will for the world and for us. "Once the soul has learned something of the will of God, there is no danger of asking for the wrong things. You find yourself asking for the kind of bread that God wants you to have."[7]

Forgive us our trespasses, as we forgive those who trespass against us. This is one petition that probably all, certainly most, Christians understand well enough: only as we forgive can we rightly ask or reasonably hope to be forgiven. (Whether we believe it or practice it as the Lord commands is another question entirely.) In no religion other than Christianity is it taught that the sinner's forgiveness of his own trespassers is the indispensable condition of God's forgiveness of the sinner. Jesus is most emphatic on the point. He gives us no reason for this divine mandate, but there has grown in my mind a very strong conviction about it: God seeks, through our praying, to foster and nurture in us a likeness to himself. Only by learning to forgive as God forgives do we learn to love as God loves.

Within the past three days, as I write this, something happened to me through somebody's carelessness that deeply offended me. It was a wrong, though done through carelessness rather than by malice. I am still angry about it, but the wrongdoer asked me to forgive him and I did—with my will. I had no right not to, as a Christian. The offense still rankles, and I told the offender that it would take some time for me to get over it; knowing myself, I know that. Some would say that if I am still angry I have not really forgiven, but I think they are wrong. Forgiveness is an expression of love, and love is an act of will.

Sometimes you have to forgive doggedly and only out of obedience; you cannot do it gleefully. But if you do it with your will, and pray that love for the offender will fully repossess your heart, you will be given growth in the very charity of God. The next time thereafter that you have to forgive, it will not be so hard, because Adam in you will have decreased and Christ in you will have increased. *That* is the answer to your prayer. Can you imagine a better one?

Lead us not into temptation, but deliver us from evil. Some thirty years ago I wrote a book in which I expressed unease about our conventional understanding of the meaning of this petition.[8] I was young then, and I am now old, but I remain of the same mind. The idea that God could deliberately lead us into temptations "to see how we can take it," as some falsely claim, is repugnant to my mind, and I am sure it is repugnant to the mind of Christ. We have not a Father in heaven who makes a game out of trying to trip us up. As James says, "God cannot be tempted by evil, nor does he tempt anyone" (Jas 1:13 NIV).

Whenever I pray for God's help against temptation, I say to God in my mind and heart: "Do not put me into situations where I must be tempted unless you give me the grace to overcome the evil." I have no doubt that this is what Jesus wants us to say to God. When I join others in the Lord's Prayer, I use the standard wording, but I do so with that mental paraphrase because I find the standard wording can be misleading. I cannot conceive of God either leading us *into* temptation, in order to test us, or leading us *away from* temptations, because they are inherent in the tasks and responsibilities he gives us to fulfill.

For that latter reason I cannot say the words of one new version of the prayer—"Save us from the time of trial"—without choking on them.[9] I know that I cannot serve God in this world, without being moved *by God himself* from one "time of trial" to another. Every moment must be a time of trial for any Christian in this world who is trying to "stand up for Jesus." Our Lord himself never ran away from tempting situations, nor did he pray to be delivered from them. He faced them squarely, and if we are his followers we must face them squarely. But knowing our own frailty, we must ask God to strengthen us for each trial and to see us through it by giving us the grace we need.

Here again, as with every petition in the Lord's Prayer,

when we pray it from our hearts it is always answered—at the very least—with the greatest and best possible gift: our becoming more like God and like Christ, more recognizable by our character as members of the divine Family into which we have been adopted. To God, and to him alone, belongs the kingdom, the power and the glory. The aim of the Lord's Prayer, and of all prayer that is begun, continued and ended in us by the Spirit, is to make us heirs of the Kingdom, instruments of the Power, partakers of the Glory and children of the Love.

17
Heaven's Preparatory Prattle

To talk about God, except in the context of prayer,
is to take His name in vain.
Ferdinand Ebner

28 MARCH. IT'S TIME TO WRAP up what I began exactly two months ago when I was moved to write this book. Looking back on what I wrote that first morning, I find that unwittingly I wrote what grew into the thesis of this essay: *When prayer passes at last into its final state of pure godliness in which God, not self, is all-in-all, it becomes that perfect adoration which is the perpetual music of heaven.* That is the result of all filial, Christian prayer which is persevered in to the End.

The ultimate answer to all prayer is God himself. The immediate answer to all prayer is growth toward God. Even "bad" prayer? Faulty, foolish, sinful prayer? Yes. But in that case it is oblique and roundabout growth, like the progress a scientific researcher might report when he has experimentally tried something and found that it doesn't work. That is growth toward the truth he seeks.

A not very bright child in school stumbles from one error to the next in his arithmetic or grammar; he's learning by his errors what are *not* the right answers. "Bad" prayers are like that, but every stumble is toward the truth rather than away from it. Pecksniff's grace is bad praying. The world—even the church—is undoubtedly full of it. But nobody bothers to pray even badly unless he or she believes there is One who hears; and that is a beginning, something on which the Holy Spirit can build. The worst of prayers provides an opening through which the Holy Spirit can get at the wretched, childish, but (perhaps unconsciously) hungry soul of the pray-er.

The creaturely prayer offered by my dog and by whales and by trees is to the glory of their Creator and must be well-pleasing in his sight. What he does with it, and with them, is between him and them. I shall not be surprised if I meet all the nonhuman creatures I have ever known, and many more, in the eternal New Order. Many of us will be disappointed if it proves not so, but in that event God will show us why we need not be.

About the filial prayer which Christ teaches, it is easier to speak confidently about those who believe that God through Christ reclaims them as his own children. For them prayer is the beginning of speech within the divine Family of which they are members forever.

The Christian on earth is an adopted infant in that Family: no more, but no less. The advanced proficient in Christ, the saint, while still in the flesh may be compared to a child of three or four in a strictly human family. The ordinary duffer of a Christian is about on the two-year-old level in his understanding and his speech, in his new life in the eternal Family. The saint is a bit ahead of the duffer but only a bit. The duffer is babyish and the saint is little-childish in the language of heaven. But both are making a start. Both, when they pray, are learning the language of heaven in the only way that any language can be learned—by using it conversationally.

A human father listening to his five-year-old son is encouraged to note that the lad is farther along than he was a year before, but he knows that he must wait for some time before he and his son can converse about space-age technology. The same father listening to the prattle of his two-year-old daughter is delighted with what he hears, especially if he can understand it. He's not at all worried because she's not yet ready to scold him for his old-fashioned ideas about art. What pleases him is that these tots are actually talking his language, even though only rudimentarily. He can wait, for they'll grow up soon enough to suit him. How much more pleased is our heavenly Father with what he hears from us!

If we want to think meaningfully about how God responds to our prayers, Jesus offers this instruction: "What man of you, if his son asks him for bread, will give him a stone? Or if he asks for a fish, will give him a serpent? If you then, who are evil, know how to give good gifts to your children, how much more will your Father who is in heaven give good gifts to those who ask him!" (Mt 7:9-11 RSV). So reads Matthew's text. Luke's is the same, except for this noteworthy difference in the closing words: " . . . how much more will the heavenly Father give *the Holy Spirit* to those who ask him!" (Lk 11:11-13 RSV). There is no conflict in meaning between "good things" and "the Holy Spirit," but the latter phrase adds much to our understanding. The good human father gives his children the best *things* he can; how much more does God give *his very own nature!*

Earlier I quoted a passage from C. S. Lewis in which he boldly suggests that when a Christian prays Christianly "he is being pulled into God, by God, while remaining himself."[1] One New Testament writer says that our destiny in Christ is to become "partakers of the divine nature" (2 Pet 1:4). In his great hymn *O God, our help in ages past,* Isaac Watts calls God himself, rather than heaven, "our eternal home," a proper paraphrase of Psalm 90:1.

God's one sure answer to any human prayer is growth either *toward* God-likeness or *in* God-likeness. It is the former if the prayer is simply a bad one; it is the latter if it is offered in faith, love, obedient self-offering, the mind of Christ. Filial prayer is the language of the new life in Christ, the language of heaven. Our best praying now is baby talk or tot talk at most. But as we persist and persevere in it we are growing into, and in, the language of God and of angels and archangels and the whole company of heaven—and our Father is well pleased with our prattle. It will not be prattle forever, and even now as we pray the Spirit is giving us growth in the only wisdom which is the knowledge and love of God, and in likeness to him of whom it is written:

From thee, great God, we spring, to thee we tend—
Path, motive, guide, original and end.[2]

Every word in that couplet is precisely true. From God we come, to God we go. He is path, motive and guide throughout our course, from our beginning at the foundation of the world to our unending end in God our eternal Home. It is through our twofold prayer of words and work that he pushes, moves and pulls us into himself, preparing us for life as his fully grown sons and daughters. With that coming of age in Christ our prayer will change from the prayer of seeking to the praise of finding: *videbimus et amabimus, amabimus et laudabimus* ("we shall see and we shall love, we shall love and we shall praise"). The classic prayer of St. Francis de Sales—"Yes, God, Yes, and always Yes!"—was his temporal anticipation (or prenatal rehearsal?) of his eternal song.

So shall it be for all who persevere in the filial prayer of the children of God unto—and into—the End.

Epilogue

They tell me, Lord, that when I seem
To be in speech with You,
Since but one voice is heard, it's all a dream,
One talker aping two.

Sometimes it is, yet not as they
Conceive it. Rather, I
Seek in myself the things I hoped to say,
But lo!, my wells are dry.

Then, seeing me empty, You forsake
The listener's role, and through
My dumb lips breathe and into utterance wake
The thoughts I never knew.

And thus You neither need reply
Nor can; thus, while we seem
Two talkers, Thou art One forever, and I
No dreamer, but Thy dream.
Author unknown

———————

Kneeling is the natural posture
for putting seeds in the ground.
Brooks Atkinson, *Once Around the Sun*

———————

O God, the Truth, make me one
with Thee in perpetual charity.
Thomas à Kempis

Notes

Chapter 1: The Morning After
[1]Logan Pearsall Smith, *Afterthoughts* (New York: Harcourt Brace Jovanovich, 1931), p. 62.
[2]Peter J. Kreeft, *Love Is Stronger Than Death* (San Francisco: Harper and Row, 1979), p. 105.

Chapter 2: Who Prays?
[1]I intend no implication as to whether a creature like Tam "goes to heaven" or "has a soul" or anything like that. I know what I firmly believe about it, but that is a subject for another book which I wish some publisher would dare me to write.
[2]This great epigram about the Incarnation is generally attributed to St. Athanasius, but it may have originated with somebody earlier.
[3]C. S. Lewis, *Mere Christianity* (London: William Collins Sons & Co., 1952), p. 148.
[4]Moral theologians have distinguished between two kinds of fear: servile fear, such as that of a slave for his master, and filial fear, such as a child's proper fear of proving unworthy of a good parent. Somewhere I have seen it defined as "a loving anxiety to please God." That is what I mean by holy fear.

Chapter 3: That Mischievous Misconception
[1]Alexis Carrel, *Prayer* (London: Hodder and Stoughton, 1947).
[2]Virgil *Aenead* 6. 376.
[3]St. Augustine *City of God* 22. 30.

Chapter 4: Vain Repetitions

[1]Quoted in *Letters to the Scattered Brotherhood,* ed. Mary Strong (New York: Harper and Row, 1948), p. 8.

Chapter 5: Pecksniffian Praying

[1]C. S. Lewis, *The World's Last Night and Other Essays* (Harcourt Brace Jovanovich, 1960), p. 9.

Chapter 7: Magical Praying

[1]G. K. Chesterton, *Orthodoxy* (New York: Dodd, Mead & Co., 1937), p. 271.

[2]Alexandre Vinet (1797-1847) was a French Protestant scholar, church reformer and man of letters. The passage here quoted may be found among his *Discourses on Certain Religious Subjects,* published in 1831 and 1841.

Chapter 8: Experience, Not Experiment

[1]James Boswell, *Life of Johnson,* 10 April 1772.

[2]The author was Mary Pickford. I am sure that she had no blasphemous intention; she was only a victim of the *Zeitgeist,* as most of us are.

[3]H. G. Wells, "Answer to Prayer," *The New Yorker* magazine, 1 May 1937.

Chapter 9: Prayer and Miracle

[1]Ivan Turgenev, "Prayer," *Dream Tales and Prose Poems* (Freeport, New York: Books for Libraries Press, 1969).

[2]Walt Whitman, *Leaves of Grass,* "Song of myself," line 31.

[3]From Charles Wesley's hymn, "Love divine, all loves excelling."

[4]Ralph Waldo Emerson, *Essays,* "Experience."

[5]The General Thanksgiving, in the offices of Morning and Evening Prayer.

[6]Samuel Taylor Coleridge, *Table Talk.*

Chapter 10: Answer or Autosuggestion?

[1]Flora Slosson Wuellner, *To Pray and to Grow* (Nashville: Abingdon Press, 1970), p. 51.

[2]I know that I have read this somewhere in Law's works, but I cannot cite the chapter and verse.

Chapter 11: God's Problem or Ours?

[1]William James, *The Will to Believe and Other Essays on Popular Philosophy* (New York: Henry Holt and Company, 1897), p. 181.

[2]The phrase *the Master of the Show* is not of Christian provenance but from the *Rubáiyát of Omar Khayyám*, trans. Edward Fitzgerald, 5th ed., verse 58. But the God of Christian faith is indeed Master of what may playfully be called "the Show"—the only show always playing.

[3]Elizabeth Barrett Browning *Aurora Leigh* 2. 95.

Chapter 12: Answers in Installments

[1]Singer said this in an interview in *The New York Times,* 3 December 1978. His full statement was: "I never say the universe was an accident. The word 'accident' should be erased from the dictionary."

[2]William Shakespeare, *Hamlet,* act 5, sc. 2, line 10.

Chapter 13: Prayer as Attention

[1]Simone Weil, *Waiting on God* (New York: G. B. Putnam's Sons, 1951), p. 68.

[2]Ibid., p. 46.

Chapter 14: Prayer and Honesty

[1]William Shakespeare, *Hamlet,* act 3, sc. 3, line 97.

[2]Oliver Wendell Holmes, *The Autocrat of the Breakfast Table,* iii.

[3]*The Book of Common Prayer,* Collect for Purity in the Order for Holy Communion.

[4]John Ruskin, *Modern Painters,* ix.

Chapter 15: Growing Pains in Prayer

[1]The phrase *sons in the Son* is St. Augustine's.

[2]Lewis, *Mere Christianity,* p. 129.

Chapter 16: The Lord's Prayer Revisited

[1]Hubert van Zeller, *Prayer in Other Words* (Springfield, Ill.: Templegate Publishers, 1963).

[2]Ibid., p. 46.

[3]Ibid., p. 48.

[4]Aldous Huxley, *The Perennial Philosophy* (New York: Harper and Row, 1945) p. 96.

[5]Van Zeller, *Prayer,* p. 48.

[6]Ibid., p. 49.

[7]Ibid., p. 50.

[8]Carroll E. Simcox, *Living the Lord's Prayer* (Morehouse-Barlow Co.), 1951.

[9]This generally appalling translation was made by an interdenominational

committee known as the International Commission on English Texts. Regrettably, it has been included in some new liturgies. It speaks well for the fundamental good sense of most rank-and-file Christians that they flatly reject it, preferring the ambiguous familiar text of this petition to the patently false one proposed as a replacement.

Chapter 17: Heaven's Preparatory Prattle

[1]Lewis, *Mere Christianity,* p. 129.

[2]This is Samuel Johnson's paraphrase of a line of Boethius and it was used as a motto for *The Rambler* (1750).